TEACHERS RESOURCES

BRITAIN
SINCE
1930

GINN
History

Contents

Introduction		**3**
The structure of Ginn History		3
The Pupils' Book		3
Oral history		4
Links with local history		4
Attainment target links		4
***Pupils' Book* notes**		**5**
The 1930s		
2/3	*Introduction*	5
4/5	*Growing up in the 1930s*	5
6/7	*Britain at work*	6
8/9	*Out of work in the 1930s*	7
10/11	*Transport and holidays*	7
12/13	*Entertainment in the 1930s*	8
The 1940s		
14/15	*The Second World War*	9
16/17	*The Blitz*	10
18/19	*The home front*	11
20/21	*After the war – 1945-50*	13
The 1950s		
22/23	*Housing in the 1950s*	13
24/25	*Growing up in the 1950s*	14
26/27	*Entertainment in the 1950s*	14
28/29	*'You've never had it so good'*	15
The 1960s		
30/31	*The swinging 60s*	15
32/33	*Growing up in the 1960s*	16
34/35	*Sport and leisure in the 1960s*	16
36/37	*Main events of the 1950s and 1960s*	17
38/39	*Emigration and immigration*	17
The 1970s and 1980s		
40/41	*Changes in work and roles*	18
42/43	*Science and invention*	19
44/45	*The environment*	19
46/47	*Looking back*	20
Key Britain Since 1930 events		**21**
Further references		**22**
Local history study		**24**
Blackline Masters		**27**

Introduction

The structure of *Ginn History*

Ginn History is a programme of work that offers a clear and continuous approach for the whole of the primary age range. It offers practical advice and resources for all areas of National Curriculum History. To resource the core study unit 'Britain Since 1930', *Ginn History* provides the following resources:

At Key Stage 1

The Key Stage 1 *Ginn History* story *A War Christmas* and the read-aloud story on pages 100 and 101 in the *Ginn History* Key Stage 1 *Teachers' Resource Book,* will give children background knowledge of the Second World War. The *Ginn History Topic Books,* and Topic Book notes on pages 39-51 of the Key Stage 1 *Teachers' Resource Book,* will introduce the children to everyday life in Britain in the recent past. The Key Stage 1 *Group Discussion Book* and the *Topic Work Group Discussion Book* provide more evidence from this period.

At Key Stage 2

The Key Stage 2 *Teachers' Handbook* provides complete support for the implementation of National Curriculum history, including guidance on curriculum planning, and full assessment and evaluation support. The *Teachers' Handbook* also contains guidance on how to teach the supplementary study units and how these units could be linked with 'Britain Since 1930'.

The *Britain Since 1930 Pupils' Book* contains full coverage of National Curriculum content areas, specifically written with the attainment targets in mind.

The *Ginn History Britain Since 1930 Group Discussion Book* is an ideal focus for discussion about this period. It is directly linked to the content areas of the *Britain Since 1930 Pupils' Book,* and it enables children to look more closely at evidence, and to investigate further source material.

The *Britain Since 1930 Teachers' Resources* is designed to support the *Pupils' Book* by providing:

- factual background information for each spread;
- suggested activities for each spread to introduce and develop historical skills and understanding, and to link to other areas of the curriculum;
- photocopiable *Blackline Master* activity sheets which help develop specific skills and act as a record for assessment;
- suggestions for covering the Supplementary Study Unit on local history through the study of 'Britain Since 1930', including a scheme of work and guidance on the resources;
- further guidance on conducting oral history;
- further references;
- a list of key 'Britain Since 1930' events.

The *Pupils' Book*

The *Britain Since 1930 Pupils' Book* examines the enormous scientific, technological, cultural and political changes that have occurred over the last 60 years. The cartoon characters in previous *Ginn History* publications are replaced by historical reminiscences from the author's family.

The materials in the book will prove useful for some of the supplementary units from list A of the National Curriculum programmes of study. For instance:

- A study of houses and places of worship will be enhanced by looking at homes throughout the period from pages 2/3 and 22/23.
- A study of domestic life, families and childhood will be able to use pages 2/3, 4/5, 12/13, 18/19, 24/25, 26/27, 32/33 and 34/35.
- Land transport themes can be extended by use of pages 10/11.

(More information on links between 'Britain Since 1930' and the supplementary units can be found in the Key Stage 2 *Teachers' Handbook*.)

Oral history

This period is the only opportunity that children following Key Stage 2 history will have for undertaking oral history.

Ideally, find people who can remember living in each decade from 1930 to 1990. These oral history respondents should be briefed so that they know what type of work the children have been doing and what they will be interested in. They should also be asked to bring in artefacts or photographs of the period. Suitable respondents may be parents, grandparents, friends, and older people from day care centres. The important point is that they can talk about things they have experienced. In areas where there is an ethnically diverse population try to get people from all groups. It may be possible to encourage those who write a language other than English to help children write a dual-language book about their visit. Ask respondents if they mind being tape recorded – even if the children take notes, they will forget!

Children should be suitably primed; they should have some open-ended questions ready. Small groups will get the best from a respondent, but if a suitable respondent can be found to talk to the whole class, this will give the children a good introduction. Children should be encouraged to write up the visit while it is still fresh in their mind. It is also worth getting children to compare different respondents' accounts of the same event. This is a good way to assess **Hi 2/3, 4** and **5**. Finally, make sure the visit finishes with a cup of tea and that the children write a thank you letter!

Links with local history

'Britain Since 1930' is an ideal vehicle for local studies and so this *Resource Book* contains a section specially devoted to that on pages 24-26.

Attainment target links

Some attainment targets have been given in detail (e.g. **En 3/2d**) whilst others have been left more open (e.g. **Te 2**) because the nature of the activity means that children may respond at a variety of levels. Where **En 3** has been identified, teachers will also have the opportunity to assess **En 4** and **En 5** if they wish. **En 1** has not been identified at every discussion point.

Pupils' Book notes

Introduction

Background information

Houses

During the 1930s about 2,500,000 houses were built. The great housing boom was stimulated by low interest rates, the movement of people towards the big cities and the need to create jobs.

The rich might live in large town or country houses. Some new houses were built in the 'mock Tudor' style, others reflected the 'Art Deco' style of the time. Rich families still had servants, though there were not so many as there were before the 1914-18 War.

Many middle-class families were able to buy their own detached or semi-detached homes. A three-bedroomed semi-detached house might cost between £500 and £800, and a mortgage of about 16s 11d (85p) compared favourably with the cost of renting – 15s 11d (80p). Most of these homes had three bedrooms, a dining room, a kitchen and a bathroom. Some had large back gardens and towards the end of the 1930s a number even had garages.

Many lower-middle-class families rented council houses. Often these were similar to the private houses, red brick being a common feature of council houses. During the 1930s the government gave local councils subsidies to build houses.

Poorer families still had to rent old Victorian terraced houses. Some back-to-backs still existed. Toilets were outside at the bottom of the yard or even shared with other families. Some families lived in just two or three rooms.

Living conditions

The National Grid was fully operational by 1931 and so gradually most houses obtained electricity. Household items like refrigerators, washing machines, televisions (after 1936) and vacuum cleaners could all be bought, but only by the richer families. Some of the new houses had built-in coppers in which the washing could be done in hot water, but the scrubbing board and the mangle were still the most common way to get the laundry done. Central heating was rare – most houses had a coal fire in each room. Modern houses had a boiler behind the kitchen or living-room fire to heat water. Floors were usually covered with linoleum (lino) and a few rugs.

Looking at evidence

There are many people who can still remember the 1930s and could bring in objects and take part in some oral history. Many of the children's families will have pictures and artefacts from the period. Even Laurel and Hardy films or others from the same period will show children the fashions of the time.

Discussion and activities

- Compare houses then with now. In what ways are they similar/different? Ask the children to list ten things that they have in their home that would not have been found in a 1930s house. **Hi 1/2c**
- Visit some nearby 1930s houses or get pictures and details from local estate agents.
- Ask the children to list ways in which houses in 1930 were an improvement on earlier (for example Tudor) houses. **Hi 1/3a**
- Discuss the photographs of housing on page 2 in the *Britain Since 1930 Group Discussion Book*.
- **BLM 1** – Interpreting evidence of the 1930s.
- **BLM 2** – Writing about 1930s housing.

Growing up in the 1930s

Background information

Elementary schools

Most children went to elementary school from the age of 5 until they were 14, when they left school. Many of these schools were old and had poor facilities. Classes were overcrowded. In 1932 government regulation set a maximum class size of 50. Teachers were much stricter then than they are today. Physical punishment was quite usual. The curriculum was dominated by the three 'R's. There were no uniforms. Boys usually wore a pair of shorts (longer than those of today) held up by braces, a woollen jumper, a shirt and knee-length woollen socks. Girls often wore a simple sleeveless shift. Those girls with long hair normally wore it in two plaits.

Grammar schools

Middle-class children often went to the grammar or secondary school at 11. They usually stayed there until they were 16 or 18 and might go on to university or to teacher training college. Others went into professions like banking and accountancy. School uniform, including a tie, was worn, and boys would have to wear a cap in the school colours. These schools were open to working-class children who could pass a scholarship at 11, but few could afford to take the place because books and the uniform had to be paid for by the family.

Private schooling

Richer families sent their children to private (that is, 'public') schools.

Childhood illness

Diseases like measles, scarlet fever, diphtheria, polio and whooping cough were still potential killers. Few children were inoculated to prevent the spread of these diseases.

Toys

Most children spent a lot of time playing outside. There were few cars then so the street was a good place to play football or cricket, or to skip and play hopscotch. Board games became increasingly popular – Monopoly originated in America but was very popular in Britain too.

Comics

Comics like *Dandy* (1937) and *Beano* (1938) started in the 1930s. Many originated in the USA, some drawing on the cinema for their heroes.

Collecting

A favourite pastime was collecting stamps or cigarette cards. Cards were put in cigarette packets and collected by children. They often went around the neighbourhood asking people if they had any old cards.

Youth organisations

Membership of youth organisations was very popular. In Britain the Boy Scouts had nearly 500,000 members and the Boys Brigade had over 160,000. The Youth Hostel Association started in 1930 and youth hostelling became a popular pastime for some. In Germany at this time the only youth organisation allowed was the Hitler Youth.

Discussion and activities

- Ask an oral history respondent about the things he or she did as a child. **Hi 3**
- Encourage the children to make a series of drawings comparing childhood now and in the 1930s. **Hi 1/2c; Ar 1**

- Using the oral history evidence and pictures from the book and newspapers, make a street frieze to act as a background for other work on the 1930s. **Hi 1/4c, 3/4**
- Ask the children to list ways in which primary schools are similar and different today, in the 1930s, and in the Victorian period. **Hi 1/2c, 3c**
- Look at the pictures of 1930s toys in the *Pupils' Book*, and on page 3 in the *Britain Since 1930 Group Discussion Book*.
- BLM 3 – Comparing 1930s and 1990s children's lifestyles.

Britain at work

Background information

After 1932 there was a slow economic recovery. During the 1930s many goods came down in price. This meant that those with a steady job had a rise in their standard of living. Before 1939 the average income was under £3.00 a week but goods then were a lot cheaper than they are now. Fuel bills were about 30p a week, a bar of Cadbury's Fruit and Nut chocolate cost 5p and bicycles could be bought for under £4.00. A new Austin Seven two-seater car cost £130 in 1930. In the mid-1930s Seebohm Rowntree's survey suggested that a family with three children could live for £2.65 per week. Working hours were long – up to ten hours a day and Saturday mornings – but most workers could look forward to a week's paid holiday during the year.

Work in the country

The drift from agricultural work continued as mechanisation increased on the farms. Tractors began to replace the horse, and even aircraft were used to spray crops.

Old industries

Many boys followed in their father's footsteps when they left school. Typically jobs depended on geographical location. The following lists the main industries in certain regions:

South Wales – coal
Lancashire – coal and cotton
North East – coal and shipbuilding
South Yorkshire – coal and iron and steel
Clydeside – iron and steel and shipbuilding
Northern Ireland – shipbuilding

These industries faced stiff competition from other European countries and from Japan. The British Empire helped the situation as members of the Empire agreed to buy British goods in return for Britain buying their produce (often food). Many of these industries were revived as Britain prepared for war.

New industries

The South East and the Midlands were the centres for the new industries. These included:

the motor car industry
the electrical industry
the chemical industry
the aircraft industry
the new consumables – furniture, chocolate, fashions.

There were also a lot of new commercial jobs in banking and offices as well as a boom in the building trade. These industries were powered by electricity so did not need to be near the coalfields. Many of these new industries used a new form of organisation called the production line. Work was often boring but it was an efficient way of manufacturing complex items.

Jobs for women

Women gradually gained a greater choice of jobs – but not the same choice as men. Many women still worked in domestic service of some kind. Women were paid lower wages than men. Married women were not allowed to work in jobs like teaching or the civil service. Most married women stayed at home to do the housework and look after the children. Labour-saving devices like the vacuum cleaner were becoming more widely available. Things like fridges were still rare, so most women had to shop nearly every day to buy fresh food.

Discussion and activities

- Ask the children to make pictures with captions showing people at work in the 1930s. **Hi 3/4; Ar 1**
- Ask your oral history respondents about the jobs they did in the 1930s. Did they think they were well off then? Do they agree with each other? **Hi 2**
- Using the 1930s prices chart on page 6 in the *Pupils' Book*, ask the children to put today's prices on items in the chart and compare the differences. **Hi 1**

8/9
Out of work in the 1930s

Background information

At the end of the 1920s the world economy was prosperous until the Wall Street crash of 1929. In the USA thousands were ruined, overseas investment was recalled and trade barriers were established. It became a vicious spiral of depression. By 1932 there were 6 million unemployed in Germany, 12 million in the USA and in Japan millions of peasant farmers were ruined. In Britain unemployment was at 3 million.

In Britain it was the areas that depended upon the old industries that were worst hit. Unemployment hit workers and the middle classes. Even banks collapsed and people lost their savings and investments. In some countries strong leadership was looked for and so the 1930s became an age of dictators – Hitler, Mussolini and Stalin are prime examples.

The Jarrow Crusade

Although conditions improved gradually after 1932, in some parts of Britain there was no improvement. In Jarrow, a shipbuilding area on the River Tyne, about 75% of the men were unemployed. In 1936, 200 men marched to London to win publicity for their plight. The town's Labour MP Ellen Wilkinson walked some of the route.

It was the threat of war that helped these people, as the old industrial skills were needed to build ships, planes and tanks.

The means test

The unemployed did receive unemployment pay (the dole) but the government was unable to meet all the demands and so in 1931 it introduced the means test. All men on the dole had to answer questions about their income (means). If they had some savings, or other people in the family had work, or even if they had some good furniture that could be sold, the dole was cut. G. K. Chesterton wrote: 'It is inhuman, it is horrible . . . People who are already clinging with their teeth and fingernails to the edge of the chasm are to be formally and legally kicked into the chasm.'

Discussion and activities

- Ask the children to discuss the plight of the unemployed and the government's response. Use Chesterton's comment here. **Hi 3/3**
- The children could draw a cartoon strip to show how the unemployed might spend their day. **Hi 3/4; Ar 1**
- Discuss the photographs on page 4 in the *Britain Since 1930 Group Discussion Book*.
- **BLM 4** – Writing about the Jarrow march.

10/11
Transport and holidays

Background information

Cars

During the 1930s the number of cars on the road doubled, from one million in 1930. By the end of the 1930s about one in ten families had a car.

Mass production brought the price of cars down substantially. There were also more accidents and so regulations were introduced. People had to pass a driving test, the speed limit in towns was fixed at 30 miles per hour, traffic signs and traffic lights were introduced, and pedestrian crossings (these were called Belisha Beacons, after the Minister of Transport Mr Hore-Belisha). Dual carriageways were built and in some countries motorways were introduced.

Other road transport

Motor bikes became increasingly popular as they were cheaper than cars. Most had a side-car to carry passengers. In towns the electric tram was the most common form of transport, though buses were becoming more common. Horses and carts were still common, as were hand carts used by street vendors. Gradually these were replaced by vans and lorries.

Aircraft

For part of the 1930s airships were thought to have a big future. They could carry people cheaply and quickly. The R101 disaster in France, in which 48 people died, ended developments in Britain. Pilots like Amy Johnson and Amelia Earhart caught the public interest in planes and by 1932 Britain's Imperial Airways were taking passengers (20 at a time) to Australia in 12 days instead of the four weeks it took by sea. However, few people could actually afford to fly by plane. For comfort most people preferred to travel by ocean liner. The *Queen Mary* and the *Queen Elizabeth* each took about five days to cross the Atlantic.

Faster and faster

During the 1930s records for distances covered and speeds travelled were broken a number of times. In Britain Sir Malcolm Campbell set the world land speed record of 500km ph (311 mph) in 1935, and the water speed record of 288km ph (179 mph) in 1939. Car racing became increasingly popular as a sport.

Seaside holidays

The gradual introduction of a week's paid annual holiday for all workers, and the ever increasing transport network, meant that many people went away from their homes for their summer holiday. Places like Margate, Scarborough, Great Yarmouth and Blackpool were increasingly popular, and more and more entertainments were put on in the resort towns.

Discussion and activities

- Make advertisements for cars that were popular in the 1930s.   **Ar 1; Hi 3**
- Some children might research the careers of heroes of the 1930s like Amy Johnson or Malcolm Campbell.   **Hi 3**
- Discuss the pictures of transport on pages 5 and 6 in the *Britain Since 1930 Group Discussion Book*.
- BLM 5 – Writing a postcard from a 1930s holiday resort.   **Hi 3; En 3**

12/13

Entertainment in the 1930s

Background information

During the 1930s more people had time and money to spend on leisure.

Radio and television

In Britain the BBC controlled all radio broadcasts. Lord Reith, the Controller of the BBC, set high standards. He believed the radio should educate as well as entertain. The announcers had to wear formal evening suits, and comedians were not allowed to make mother-in-law jokes. The most popular times for listening were midday and the early evening. Favourite programmes were variety, dance music and sport. Many children listened to *Children's Hour*, which was introduced by an 'Auntie' or an 'Uncle'. There was no commercial radio, though it was possible to pick up stations from Luxembourg and Ireland.

BBC television began broadcasting in 1936 to the London area. TV shut down for the duration of the war.

The cinema

Many people went to the cinema regularly. The movies were now 'talkies', and a whole host of new stars became popular like Laurel and Hardy, Clark Gable, Vivien Leigh, Leslie Howard, Judy Garland, Shirley Temple, Marlene Dietrich, Greta Garbo, Charles Laughton, Ronald Coleman, Errol Flynn, the Marx Brothers, Jean Harlow and Katherine Hepburn. Walt Disney was popular, with favourites like Snow White, Mickey Mouse and Pluto.

The centre of the industry was Hollywood. American slang spread, and the cinema influenced fashions and hairstyles. From 1934 a code was adopted so that love always ended in marriage, and crime never paid. The cinema was good value – two feature-length films and a newsreel for as little as 2p. It was even cheaper on a Saturday morning when children's matinees were run (for example *Flash Gordon* or *Tarzan*). The cinema outstripped the music hall, but the halls were still very popular.

Sport

The biggest spectator sports were football and cricket. Arsenal was the top football club and the English team reckoned itself the best in the world. Cricket was very popular, especially the Ashes series against Australia. The 1933 Tests nearly caused an international incident when Harold Larwood (England) bowled at the Australians' bodies. The Australians thought that 'bodyline bowling' was unsporting.

Famous sports personalities included Jesse Owens, Donald Bradman, Len Hutton, Joe Louis, Fred Perry and Helen Wills Moody. Gambling on sport became increasingly popular and the 'pools' was a great industry.

Music

Dancing to swing bands was a popular pastime. Band leaders like Ambrose, Billy Cotton and Henry Hall were the stars. Bing Crosby was popular, as were George Formby and Gracie Fields.

In the 1930s there were many dance-halls. Formal dances such as the foxtrot and waltz were popular.

Books and newspapers

Reading really took off in the 1930s. For newspapers it was a golden age. Their circulations were so high that advertising alone paid for the paper. In 1935 Penguin paperbacks were launched – they sold for 6d each. The crime stories of Agatha Christie and Dorothy Sayers were especially popular. The story of the Abdication was followed by many people through the newspapers and on the radio.

Discussion and activities

- Compare the 1930s radio programme (on page 12) with a Radio 1 programme today.
- Get the children to carry out their own investigations into the stars or a famous football club of the 1930s.   **Hi 3**
- Ask oral history respondents about their 1930s idols.
- Record some old 1930s films and show them to the children as evidence of fashion, transport, etc.
- Look at the photograph of a dance-hall on page 7 in the *Britain Since 1930 Group Discussion Book*.

Background information

The beginning of the war

The bitterness that many Germans felt as a result of the First World War and the Depression provided the background for the rise of Hitler and the Nazi party. Hitler was determined to unite all the German areas of Europe into one large state. In 1938 he took over Austria and threatened Czechoslovakia. The British Prime Minister, Neville Chamberlain, thought that war with Germany would be disastrous for Britain, even if we won. (He was proved right.) He tried to appease Hitler. In September 1938 Hitler, Chamberlain, Daladier (France) and Mussolini (Italy) met at Munich. At Munich it was agreed that Hitler could take over the German-speaking part of Czechoslovakia (the people who lived there wanted this). Chamberlain declared that he had established 'Peace for our time'. In March 1939 Hitler took over the rest of Czechoslovakia and threatened that part of Poland that divided Germany in two. Britain and France warned Hitler that if he attacked Poland they would declare war. On 1st September he attacked Poland. On 3rd September 1939 Britain and France declared war on Germany.

German tactics

The Germans used a tactic called *blitzkrieg* – a lightning-fast attack by tanks, motorised infantry and planes. They quickly defeated the large Polish army.

Churchill

On the day that the German offensive was launched through western Europe, Chamberlain resigned. Winston Churchill was made Prime Minister. He was already 65 but had supported the idea of war in the 1930s. He had had a very mixed political career to date. As Britain stood alone he made a number of stirring speeches:

'We shall defend our island whatever the cost may be. We shall fight on the beaches, we shall fight on the landing grounds, we shall fight in the fields and in the streets, we shall fight in the hills . . . we shall never surrender.'

'Let us brace ourselves to our duties, and so bear ourselves that, if the British Empire and Commonwealth last for a thousand years men will say, "This was their finest hour".'

The Phoney War

Over the winter of 1939-40 there was little fighting. The French stayed in their strong defences (the Maginot Line), and were supported by a small British force. The British navy quickly achieved superiority at sea.

Hitler strikes

The Germans attacked and overran Denmark and Norway in April 1940. In May, German forces overran Belgium, the Netherlands and northern France. The British army was cut off and surrounded on the French coast – it looked as if it must surrender.

Dunkirk

At the end of May and the start of June, hundreds of boats sailed from Britain to the French coast and rescued the Allied forces from the beaches of Dunkirk. Almost anything that could float, even if it could only carry a few soldiers, helped the navy. Over 300,000 Allied troops were rescued.

The Battle of Britain

Beaches and roads in Britain were lined with barbed wire and guarded. Road signs were taken down. The home guard was established as a defence force. Some of these men prepared to fight off Hitler's troops with pitchforks and broomsticks!

Hitler was not prepared to attack Britain by sea because of the strength of the British navy, so he tried to weaken Britain by dominating the skies. The German Luftwaffe was confident that it would destroy the RAF, which was much weaker at this stage of the war. From July to September a vital battle was fought in which the British Spitfires and Hurricanes kept the Luftwaffe at bay. Churchill praised the pilots: 'Never was so much owed by so many to so few.'

The war effort

All men between 18 and 43 except special workers (for example shipbuilders and some coal miners) were conscripted into the armed services if they were fit enough. This meant that many factories were short of workers, so women filled these gaps. They also volunteered for the armed forces. Factories changed their production lines – tanks were made instead of cars, and at Bourneville anti-aircraft rockets were made instead of chocolate. Even children helped by collecting scrap iron for the manufacture of weapons.

World War

Britain always had the support of the Empire but in 1941 Germany attacked Russia, and Japan attacked the USA. Britain was now at war with Japan but was allied with Russia and the USA. In early 1942 it looked as if the Germans and Japanese would continue their success. In the autumn of 1942 the tide turned. The Russians finally stopped the Germans and defeated them, and in North Africa British forces defeated the combined Italian and German army. Throughout 1943-44 the British/American alliance built up its forces for an attack on France. On 6th June 1944 the Allies landed on the beaches of Normandy. D-day had arrived. Gradually the Germans were pushed back, and the war was nearly over.

Discussion and activities

- Using an atlas index, find Germany, Czechoslovakia, Belgium, the Netherlands, Norway, Poland and France, and locate them on a map.
  Gg 1/4e
- Watch a video of *Dad's Army*, which depicted a humorous view of the home guard. Discuss the clothes and the weapons, and the role of people like the ARP Warden.
- Oral history respondents or the children's own families might have pictures of themselves in the armed forces – these can provide evidence for an examination of the forces of the time.
- Discuss the pictures of the war effort on page 8 in the *Britain Since 1930 Group Discussion Book*.
- **BLM 6** – Looking at a wartime identity card, and designing a 1990s comparison.
- **BLM 7** – Looking at wartime jobs.

16/17

The Blitz

Background information

Gas masks

Children had special masks with a red 'beak' in front. Babies had airtight containers into which filtered air was pumped using hand bellows. Children had to practise wearing their masks at school. Most people thought they were nasty, rubbery things. They were supposed to be carried at all times but gradually people began to leave them at home.

Evacuation

The government asked parents to send children away to safety. About four million people were a priority for evacuation: school-aged children and their teachers, pre-school children and their mothers, expectant mothers and the blind. Evacuees began moving out of the big cities on 1st September 1939 – two days before war was declared. It was thought that the war would start with an immediate bombing campaign.

Although large numbers of children left cities, large numbers also stayed behind. In London about 50% went, in Liverpool and Manchester about 60% but in Sheffield only about 15%. By January 1940 many had returned home, although when bombing really started some went away again. Most evacuees went to smaller towns and villages but some went as far as Canada. Children's experiences of evacuation are very mixed. Some were made very welcome, others were treated badly. Some of the evacuees were very poor, and middle-class families were appalled at the condition of their clothing, their manners and personal hygiene. Some children were well received by local families but not liked by the local children! Local schools often doubled their numbers and some had to work shift systems. For the children it was a remarkable experience – many had never been to the country before.

The blackout

The blackout was meant to make it harder for German bombers to find their targets. Windows had to be covered when inside lights were on. Street lights and car lights were reduced to the minimum. Many windows were also covered with sticky brown Xs to stop them being blown out by explosions.

Air raids

A sharp contrast to the dark on the ground was the searchlights directed up at German planes. The bombing of Britain began in May 1940. The first bombs dropped on a city fell on London in August 1940. The blitz of London and other cities started in September. London, Coventry and Plymouth were among the worst hit, closely followed by Liverpool, Hull, Bristol, Southampton, Portsmouth and Glasgow.

Shelters

Many Londoners spent their nights in the Underground to escape the worst of the bombing. During September 1940 up to 177,000 people were sleeping underground. Other people used Anderson or Morrison shelters. The programme for building Anderson shelters began in 1938. Essentially it was a reinforced corrugated iron hut half buried in the garden and covered with 40-50cm of earth. They proved to be good protection for up to six people. Over 20 million of these were built. Many people sheltered at home, under the stairs, in cupboards, under tables or in properly made Morrison shelters. This was a strong metal mesh box. It could be put in the living-room and used as a table. One side could be lifted up for people to crawl into the shelter.

Flying bombs

After the Blitz, Hitler concentrated on Russia. It was not until 1944 that Britain came under sustained attack again. During 1944 many children were evacuated once more as over 1,000 V2 rockets were launched.

Bombing of German cities

It is important to remember that the bombing of cities was carried out by the Allies as well. In fact German cities suffered much more than British cities – this is one of the factors that contributed to the Allied victory.

Discussion and activities

- An ideal mix of oral history respondents would be an evacuee and someone who received evacuees. Discuss with the children whether the respondents' views on evacuation are similar. **Hi 2, 3**
- Ask the children to design a survival kit to keep in a shelter. **Te**
- There are many stories about evacuees, including the *Ginn History War Christmas* read-aloud story (on page 100 in the Key Stage One *Teachers' Resource Book*). Read one of these to the children and get them to write their own account of evacuation. This work should be combined with a study of the many excellent photographs of evacuees that are available. **En 3; Hi 3**
- Use Front Page Xtra or a similar computer programme to write a newspaper article about an air raid. **Te 5, En 3**
- Look at the pictures of air raid warnings, shelters, and bomb damage on pages 9-11 in the *Britain Since 1930 Group Discussion Book*.
- Your school log book may be a valuable source of information about evacuees, air raid practices and school life during the war.
- **BLM 8** – Looking at evacuation.

18/19

The home front

Background information

Food shortages

German U-boats (submarines) effectively cut Britain off from outside supplies of food. Service men and women were the priority for food. At home there were many shortages though people were encouraged to 'Dig for Victory', to grow their own vegetables. Farmers were encouraged to be more efficient and pastureland was turned over to crops. British food production increased massively and waste was discouraged. Lord Woolton, Minister of Food, made up this rhyme:

'Those who have the will to win
Cook potatoes in their skin
Knowing that the sight of peelings
Deeply hurts Lord Woolton's feelings.'

Every morning the radio gave housewives a short talk on how to make the best of a little food.

Rationing

From January 1940 food rationing was introduced to make sure it was shared out fairly. Everyone had a ration book containing coupons. People had to register with a particular shop. Shopkeepers then tore out coupons in return for food. Butter, jam, sugar, bacon, ham and sweets were all rationed. Children were allowed two ounces (57g) of sweets a week. As the war went on the food ration varied but became smaller. A typical weekly ration for one person was as follows:

4oz (100g) cheese
4oz (100g) bacon
2oz (50g) butter
2oz (50g) cooking fat
2oz (50g) margarine
8oz (225g) sugar
4oz (100g) jam
2oz (75g) sweets
2oz (50g) tea (adults only)
approximately ¾lb (350g) of minced beef
or meat of equivalent value
1 fresh egg (3 for children)
3 eggs as dried egg powder
7 pints of milk for children under 5
3½ pints of milk for school-age children (most of whom also had school milk)
1 pint's worth of dried milk

Many food items like meat and fruit were not rationed for periods but were very difficult or expensive to get. Substitutes like dried eggs could be used in cake making. As a result of food rationing, many people had healthier diets than before the war.

Clothes were also rationed from 1941. People were encouraged to 'make do and mend'. People had between 48 and 66 coupons a year. A man could only buy a new jacket every two years. Children's clothes were rated like this:

Item	Number of coupons
Mackintosh	7
Blazer	8
Jumper	3
Trousers	6
Dress	5
Shirt	4
Underpants/knickers	2
Shoes	3
Pair of socks	1
Skirt	5
Pair of gloves	2

The poor suffered more because they started off with a poorer stock of clothes. Clothes were patched and re-used. They were also swapped and re-sold.

Other rationed items included petrol, coal and soap. Other savings were made too, for example the size of newspapers was reduced, and the amount of water allowed for a bath. People were encouraged to save bottles, paper, bones, scrap metal and rags. Children collected these for recycling.

Most things could be obtained if you could pay. 'Spivs' did a good trade in items like stockings.

Government propaganda

People were eager to know how the war was going, so the radio and newspapers were popular. The government set up a Ministry of Information to make sure that the media did not pass on any vital information to the Germans, or give the British people depressing news. Morale was good and the government manipulated the news and even the cinema to keep spirits high. People were encouraged not to gossip in case enemy agents over heard them, they were told: 'Careless talk costs lives'.

Leisure

Social life did not stop because of the war. People went to dances which were even more popular once the American GIs came here, to the cinema and the pub. The radio was a popular form of entertainment – ITMA (It's That Man Again) was a cult radio comedy that almost everybody listened to. Occasions like weddings were still celebrated, though often with a cardboard cake!

The end of the war

After the success of D-day, Allied troops under Eisenhower re-took France, Belgium and the Netherlands, and pushed into western Germany. Meanwhile the Russians invaded Germany from the east. Hitler committed suicide on 30th April 1945 and Germany surrendered a week later. On 8th May (VE Day – Victory in Europe) there was great rejoicing with street parties. Japan continued to fight on but in August atom bombs were dropped on Hiroshima and Nagasaki. Thousands died. Japan surrendered.

The war had cost Britain nearly 400,000 lives. There were serious shortages, the economy was weak and the USA was owed a great deal of money. The invention of the atomic bomb made the threat of another war even more horrible.

Discussion and activities

- Compile a list with the children of a typical week's war ration. Ask them to try to plan a menu with it.
  Te; Hi 3
- Discuss with the children the censorship of news. Do the children think the government was right to censor news during the war?
- Interview oral history respondents who were at home during the war.
- Allow the children to make their own propaganda posters. **Te**
- Ask the children to make their own booklet on the home front based on a variety of evidence.
  Hi 1/4c, 3/3, 4; En 3
- Look at the photograph of ration books on page 12 in the *Britain Since 1930 Group Discussion Book*.

- Discuss the photographs of servicemen returning from the war on page 13 in the *Britain Since 1930 Group Discussion Book*. How would these men and their families have felt? Discuss the fact that many servicemen did not return.
- **BLM 9** – Writing diary entries about the Blitz.
- **BLM 10 and 11** – Looking at wartime rationing and how best to use personal food and clothing allowances.
- **BLM 12** – Points of view about the atom bomb.

After the war – 1945-50

Background information

Things were not immediately better after the war: there had been huge economic and human cost; Britain was in debt as she had lost many of her markets; old machinery in factories had not been replaced; exports had to be high to earn money for the necessary raw materials; thousands of service men had to be got back into civilian life. Shortages continued and rationing of food, paper, coal, clothing and petrol continued.

Massive home building was needed to replace bomb damage. Temporary prefabricated buildings (prefabs) were put up – there are still some families living in these temporary homes today!

The Welfare State

After the war there was a general election which the Labour party won as they seemed to have the best policies for the future. The Conservatives under Winston Churchill had rested on Churchill's war record. Churchill's wartime government had set up a commission under William Beveridge to make a report on poverty. Beveridge thought it was the government's job to look after people from the cradle to the grave. From this report stemmed the 'Welfare State'. Alongside this the Labour Government enforced a policy of nationalisation – the major industries and services were placed under government control.

Discussion and activities

- Ask the children why they think Winston Churchill was voted out of office. **Hi 3**
- Discuss with the children the policies the Labour Government introduced between 1945 and 1950. Which of these policies do the children think is the most important?

Housing in the 1950s

Background information

Housing

The 1950s opened with a serious housing shortage. During the 1950s house building reached new records. Many new estates were built on the edge of towns and some entirely new towns were built. Many of the new houses were owned by the local councils who rented them to people (council houses) but others were privately owned. Blocks of flats were also becoming a feature. Some of these were low-rise, but many were high-rise tower blocks. They made good use of the available land, were quickly assembled from factory-made units, had good amenities like central heating, and provided a quick solution to the housing problem. They also had disadvantages: people felt isolated; many old people and those with young families were virtually prisoners in their own homes; it was hard to meet the neighbours; and there were practical difficulties to solve such as bikes, cars and rubbish. Some tower blocks were so badly built that they had to be demolished in the 1960s and 70s.

Living conditions

The new tower blocks had central heating and so did the more expensive privately owned houses but most homes were still heated by coal fires. This meant that parts of the house were warm but other parts, bedrooms especially, were very cold. All new houses were built with inside bathrooms and toilets and some conversions were carried out on older properties. Most houses now had gas or electric cookers. Washing machines and refrigerators became more common, as did television. Cleaning the house, feeding and clothing the family all became slightly easier than it was in the 1930s.

Discussion and activities

- Visit some 1950s houses or flats. Compare them with 1930s and modern houses. **Hi 1/3c**
- Ask the children to list their ideas about the pros and cons of high-rise living.
- Ask the children to bring in artefacts to set up a 1950s museum. Encourage them to research the items they bring in and make informative museum labels'. **Hi 3**

Growing up in the 1950s

Background information

Schools

The baby boom following the war meant that there was a severe shortage of school places and of teachers. Many new schools were built. They were more pleasant than 1930s schools. They often had plenty of windows, large playgrounds and playing fields. Teacher were still strict – the cane was still used. The main curriculum concern was still the three 'R's, though some geography, history and art and craft were taught. Streaming was common in primary and secondary modern schools. Even grammar schools streamed their children. The Eleven Plus (11+) exam aimed to sort out the children most likely to benefit from different kinds of education. A grammar school education was seen as best – secondary modern schools were supposed to be more vocational. The 11+ exam tested for English, maths and intelligence. Approximately 20% of children passed into the grammar school system. Some LEAs introduced technical schools which were supposed to provide higher vocational training.

The one thing everybody from this era seems to remember is school milk! Each child was allowed a third of a pint, in a bottle. This was a measure to help make children healthier, as was the introduction of school dinners. A school dinner might cost a shilling (12d) a day.

National Service

Britain was allied with the USA and the countries of western Europe against what was seen as the communist threat from Russia and eastern Europe. To keep the services at full strength all men had to spend two years in the services when they reached the age of 18. The period 1945-61 is the only time in Britain's peacetime history when men have been forced to serve in the services. Some people saw this as desirable in the way it instilled discipline and respect and 'made a man of you'. Many of the young men certainly enjoyed their service life, though others did not. During this time British servicemen were active in West Germany, Egypt, Cyprus, and in many parts of the Commonwealth.

Discussion and activities

- Allow the children to try writing using old 'dip-nib' pens.
- Interview someone who went to school in the 1950s. What do they remember? Use this and other evidence to write about schools in the 1950s. **Hi 3/4**
- Organise a class debate on either the 11+, or conscription and National Service. **En 1**

- Look at the pictures of grammar and secondary modern schools on page 14 in the *Britain Since 1930 Group Discussion Book.*

Entertainment in the 1950s

Background information

Radio and television

Radio (wireless) was still very popular throughout the 1950s. Shows like *The Goon Show, The Navy Lark* and *Hancock's Half Hour* were popular comedies, there were thrillers like *Dick Barton* and even popular serials (soaps!) like *Mrs Dale's Diary* and *The Archers*. In 1954 audiences were about 9 million but by 1957 they were down to about 6 million. Television had arrived!

Two events gave television an impetus. The Coronation of Queen Elizabeth in 1953 was televised and many new sets were sold and new transmitters set up. Up to 25 million people probably watched the Coronation. The second boost was the introduction of ITV in 1956.

The first TV advert was for Gibbs SR toothpaste. For a while ITV seemed to have the better programmes for children and adults – their quiz shows were especially popular. TV made an enormous change to family life. By 1959 most families had a TV and many watched it for more than four hours a day. Children spent much less time playing outside and less time reading. Many cinemas were forced to close down because of the lack of business.

Sport

Football and cricket still attracted large crowds though many of the major sporting events were now shown on television. More facilities for people to take part in sport were made available.

Reading

During the 1950s public libraries in Britain were very popular. Often whole families went together to choose books. The sale of paperbacks had topped 60 million by 1958. This was the era of Ian Fleming's James Bond books for adults, and Enid Blyton for children.

Discussion and activities

- Organize the children into groups, each collecting different data about television viewing. Areas to investigate could include:

- popularity of programmes
- popularity of channels
- time spent viewing.

They can then find suitable ways to communicate this data, and compare evidence about 1950 television viewing with their findings. **Ma 5**

- Ask children to research particular people from the 1950s, such as Stanley Matthews, The Goons, Enid Blyton, etc. **Hi 3**
- Ask oral history respondents to talk about the Coronation and some of their favourite moments from 1950s TV.
- Look at the photographs of 1950s children's television programmes on page 15 in the *Britian Since 1930 Group Discussion Book*.
- BLM 13 – Designing an advertisement for a 1950s television set.

28/29

'You've never had it so good'

Background information

Prosperity

The Labour Government had done much to rebuild Britain and had introduced the Welfare State, but rationing continued and in 1948 rations were smaller than in the war. In 1951 Churchill (Conservative) was re-elected, but in 1954 he resigned and was replaced by Sir Anthony Eden. Eden resigned in 1957 after the 'Suez Affair' and was replaced by Harold Macmillan. As the 1950s progressed people were better fed, housed and clothed than at any previous time. They owned more goods and spent more on leisure and consumables. World trade picked up, but much of the hard work was now done by machines. Most people now worked an eight-hour day for five days a week and had two weeks' paid holiday. There was full employment. Goods that had seemed to be luxuries like televisions, washing machines and refrigerators became commonplace. Mass production brought prices down and credit facilities made purchasing easier.

Cars

More and more people bought their own cars, largely British-made like the Ford Anglia, Consul and Zephyr, and the Morris Minor and Oxford. Britain's first motorways, the M1 and the M6, were built at the end of the 1950s.

Teenagers

The term 'teenager' was first used in the 1950s. Young people had money and did not want to conform to the model of their parents. Fashions were made especially for teenagers. The lasting image of the 1950s is the teddy boy. This was a reversion to Edwardian fashions with tight drainpipe trousers, brocaded waistcoats, narrow ties, and long jackets trimmed with velvet. Teddy boys wore 'winkle-picker shoes' that were very pointed at the toe. Hair was groomed carefully with Brylcreem. However, most men were not teddy boys, and wore sports jackets and flannel trousers. Ties were frequently worn. The girls' skirts tended to be flared, with a tight waistband. Stiletto-heeled shoes were also popular.

Teenage music

Teenagers developed their own music during the 1950s. Previously they had listened to the same music as their parents. The first big rock 'n' roll hit was *Rock Around the Clock* by Bill Haley and the Comets. Elvis Presley, Little Richard and Buddy Holly were the big stars but so were some British singers like Tommy Steele, Lonny Donegan, Marty Wilde and Cliff Richard. Many teenagers liked to go to coffee bars, play the juke box and jive.

Discussion and activities

- Allow the children to make drawings or collages to show fashions of the period. These should be compared with fashion now. They could be added to a frieze of a coffee bar. **Hi 1/4c; Ar 1**
- Ask the children to do some research on individual pop singers, writers, politicians or musicans.
- See if any of your oral history respondents will teach or show the children how to jive.
- Discuss with the children whether or not Harold Macmillan's assertion that people had 'never had it so good' was right. **Hi 2**
- Record some TV programmes or films set in the 1950s (like *Happy Days*). Watch these programmes, looking at the fashion and listening to the music.
- Play the children a selection of 50s music. **Mu 2**
- Discuss the pictures on page 16 in the *Britain Since 1930 Group Discussion Book*.
- BLM 14 – Looking at teenage leisure in the 1950s.

30/31

The swinging 60s

Background information

Until the 1960s the leading pop singers were American. That changed with the arrival of the Beatles in 1962-63. Beatlemania swept the country as the 'Fab Four' recorded hit after hit. They put on many concerts for which people queued for hours. Then the audiences went wild with excitement. Beatlemania soon swept the world. Other stars soon followed in their footsteps – The Searchers, Gerry and the Pacemakers, Cilla Black, Billy J Kramer all came from Liverpool too. Other popular groups were the Dave Clarke Five, The Animals, Herman's Hermits and The Kinks. Some groups set out to show a more rebellious side of youth – The Rolling Stones and The Who. Some singers like Bob Dylan sang songs to protest about the way the older generation were running the world. Cliff Richard had the most 1960s hits (43).

Fashion

New, cheaper materials and a wave of imaginative designers produced a huge variety of changes to fashion in the 1960s. The mini-skirt probably symbolises the fashion changes. Skirt hems gradually rose higher and higher, coinciding with the introduction of tights in place of stockings. At various times long hair and back-combed hair were fashionable, men's clothes became more colourful, and by the end of the 1960s jeans and T-shirts were popular. London became the fashion capital of the world. The small boutiques along Carnaby Street and later the King's Road were the centre of the industry. Designers like Mary Quant and models like Twiggy led the way.

Mods, rockers and hippies

Many teenagers adopted a particular look and music. This was reflected in their style of life. The newspapers often carried reports of their rebellious behaviour and the fights that broke out between mods and rockers at seaside resorts.

Discussion and activities

- Play some music from the time. Use material from the early and later Beatles periods, play The Rolling Stones and some protest songs.   **Mu 2**
- Ask the children to investigate the popularity of different pop groups of the period. They should design their own questionnaire and find ways of communicating their findings.   **Ma 5; Hi 3**
- Get the children to make a display of pictures and captions to show the changing fashions of the 1960s.
  Hi 3; Ar 1
- Look at the photographs of the swinging 60s on page 17 in the *Britain Since 1930 Group Discussion Book*.
- BLM 15 – Designing a record sleeve for a 1960s record.

┌──── 32/33 ────┐
Growing up in the 1960s
└───────────────┘

Background information

Many young people lived very different lives to their parents. Higher education had expanded and many now lived away from home at universities and colleges. Many younger people thought that their parents' generation was not making a good job of running the world and there were protests about the way higher education was run, about Vietnam, apartheid and the Bomb. By 1969 there were 300,000 students in higher education, twice the number of the 1950s. Teenagers and those in their twenties were in a stronger position than ever before. Because of the post-war baby boom there were more of them and they had more money and consumer power than previous generations. This was reflected in the change in the law in 1969 allowing everyone over the age of 18 the vote.

Changes in education

In the early 1960s the culture of protest extended to the 11+ system. Many thought it was unfair that people's lives could be so deeply affected by an exam at the age of 11. In 1965 the Labour Government ordered LEAs to abolish the 11+ and to introduce comprehensive schools. During the 1960s there were other great changes in schools. There were more language laboratories, record players, tape recorders and televisions, and project work became fashionable.

Discussion and activities

- Pop groups and singers set many of the fashions in the 1960s. Who do the children think sets the fashion today?
- Ask oral history respondents about the 11+ and about their schooling. Do they think the 11+ was a good idea?   **Hi 2, 3**
- What would children like to protest about today? What would be the best ways to make an effective protest? Allow the children to make posters and banners about issues that they feel are important today.
- BLM 16 – Identifying the reasons for the introduction of comprehensive schools.
- BLM 17 – Describing teenage leisure time in the 1950s and 1960s.

┌──── 34/35 ────┐
Sport and leisure in the 1960s
└───────────────┘

Background information

Bingo halls

As television became even more popular, fewer and fewer people went to the cinema. In 1960 bingo became legal and many old cinemas re-opened as bingo halls.

Pop and the radio

Pop music played an important part in young people's lives. Many of them owned record players, and sales of singles were higher than today. Most young people had small portable transistor radios. Radio Luxembourg was popular because the BBC did not cater for pop music. Radio Caroline was a 'pirate' (illegal) radio station but that too was very popular. It began broadcasting in 1964 from a ship off the Essex coast. In 1967 the BBC introduced Radio 1 to play non-stop pop. Among others, Tony Blackburn, Jimmy Saville and Kenny Everett, became famous as Radio 1 DJs.

Sport and leisure

Thanks to TV, millions of people saw the great sporting moments of the 60s. Sports personalities like Bobby Charlton, George Best (football), Freddie Trueman (cricket) and Ann Jones (tennis) could be watched in their moments of triumph. So could some of the famous teams – none more famous than the 1966 English World Cup team. There were many other sporting activities like squash and golf available to everyone as new facilities were opened. Ten-pin bowling was popular for a time but had died out by the end of the 60s only to become popular again in the 1990s. The traditional sports of football and cricket became less popular with spectators. The cricket authorities introduced the one-day game to attract more spectators.

More money meant people could travel abroad for holidays. Package holidays to Spanish resorts were affordable for many people who had never been abroad before. Fast-food chains like Wimpy became popular and so did take-away food from Indian and Chinese restaurants.

Supermarkets expanded considerably, at the expense of corner shops. Now people were able to shop on a weekly basis rather than every day.

Discussion and activities

- The children could conduct their own research on some of the famous sporting personalities. They may wish to look beyond Britain at Americans like Cassius Clay. **Hi 3**
- See if the children can find out which 1960s films and television programmes are still popular today. **Hi 1/4a**

36/37
Main events of the 1950s and 1960s

Background information

The *Pupils' Book* concentrates on young people and popular culture during the 1950s and 1960s. These pages give a selection of the major events of the period. Any list is bound to leave out some events, but this is a good way of illustrating AT2.

Discussion and activities

- Ask the children to make their own time lines of the 1950s and 60s. Restrict them to choosing one world event, one British event and one family event for each year, to help them realise how selective historians are. **Hi 2, 3**
- The children can then make a line for the last ten years using the same categories. **Hi 2, 3**
- The children could conduct a survey of which events are best remembered by people who were alive during the 1950s and 1960s. Does their age make any difference? **Ma 5**
- Look at the newspaper articles and photographs of the Aberfan disaster on pages 18 and 19 in the *Britain Since 1930 Group Discussion Book*.

38/39
Emigration and immigration

Background information

The British Empire

In the 1930s the British Empire amounted to about a quarter of the world's surface. The word 'Commonwealth' was first used after the First World War to describe the links between Canada, Australia, South Africa, New Zealand and Britain. They had been running their own affairs since before the First World War.

After the Second World War most countries in the Empire won the right to rule themselves. In 1947 India and Pakistan gained independence. In 1957 the first African state – Ghana – became independent. By the early 1960s most countries within the Empire had become independent. They included Malaysia, Singapore, Nigeria, Cyprus, Sierra Leone, Tanzania, Jamaica, Trinidad and Tobago, Uganda, Kenya and Malawi. Although they were no longer ruled by Britain, most still remained within the Commonwealth and accepted Queen Elizabeth as Head of State.

Today little remains of the Empire except a few small islands including the Falkland Islands. In 1982 Argentina attacked and invaded the Falklands. Armed forces were used to recapture it.

Even the United Kingdom might not hold together. Some people in Northern Ireland want to belong to Eire, and there are strong home rule movements in Scotland and Wales.

Emigration

Even today more people emigrate from Britain than come into it. Historically destinations have been Australia, New Zealand and Canada. Now the USA and Europe can be added to that list.

Immigration

In 1948 a British Nationalities Act made all Commonwealth citizens 'Citizens of the United Kingdom and the Colonies'. The 1950s and 60s saw a large number of black immigrants from the Caribbean and from India and Pakistan come to Britain. During the 1950s employers like British Rail, London Underground and the National Health Service were very short of labour and actively recruited in the Caribbean for workers. The 1960s saw a number of attempts to slow down the rate of immigration.

Racial tension

Immigrants often settled in particular parts of Britain and in certain areas of cities. Often this depended on the availability of jobs, of cheap housing, and the need to develop a community spirit. Immigrants in Britain were subjected to a great deal of discrimination, some of it very open but some institutional. In 1958 there were riots in Notting Hill and in the early 1980s, there were disturbances in Brixton. The Swann educational report (1979) and the Scarman report showed how disadvantaged black people were in education and in life in general. In 1968 the Race Relations Act made racial discrimination illegal. Even so, many black British people still suffer discrimination today.

Multicultural Britain

Most towns and cities include people from different ethnic groups. Across the whole country new ideas, music and food have spread as a result of the diversity of Britain's people.

The European Community

In 1957 six countries joined together to form the European Economic Community. Following a referendum, Britain joined the EEC in 1973. Now Britain has more trade with its European partners than with the Commonwealth.

Discussion and activities

- Ensure that some of your oral history respondents for this period are from the black community. Where appropriate they may like to help the children to write dual-language booklets about their past. **En 3**
- Get the children to use an atlas with an index to find and locate the countries in the old Empire. **Gg 1/4e**
- Get the children to find the members of today's European Community in an atlas. **Gg 1/4e**

Changes in work and roles

Background information

Automation

Workplaces have changed considerably during the last 30 years. In factories, in particular, much of the hard labour is now done by machines. These are often programmed and can almost run themselves. Although this has improved conditions it has also meant that more people have become unemployed. Those industries that have not become automated produce expensive goods and have been undersold by competition, especially from Japan and Germany. This has contributed to unemployment.

Trade unions

Immediately after the war the trade unions were strong. They managed to win better conditions and higher wages for their workers. As competition became harder and unemployment higher they tried to protect jobs and to get higher wages. The demand for higher wages helped fuel inflation which made British goods uncompetitive. In the 1970s miners and power workers went on strike. Electricity was cut off and some working days were lost. In 1974 the Conservative Government under Edward Heath was not re-elected after a strike by coal miners. The winter of 1978-79 saw lots of strikes – dustmen, hospital workers, grave diggers – and people called it the 'Winter of Discontent'. The Labour Government of James Callaghan was defeated by the Conservatives under Margaret Thatcher. She was determined to reduce the power of the unions. New laws were passed. The real battle came in 1984-85 when the miners went on strike. This was a very bitter confrontation between the miners and the government but the government refused to give ground and the miners eventually went back to work.

Women and paid employment

The greatest change in the workforce over the period has been the growing number of women who are in paid employment. The war had done much to get women into work and despite a lull in the 1950s more women are now working. In the 1950s and 1960s most unmarried women worked and gradually those with grown-up children rejoined the labour market. From the 1970s onwards women with pre-school or school-aged children have also worked. In some cases the increase in working women has been an economic necessity for their families but in others women have wanted to pursue their careers. Gradually women are winning the right to equal pay and to equality of opportunity.

Despite being in paid employment many women are still the major carers in their families.

Discussion and activities

- Ask the children to list the good effects and the bad effects of automation.   **Hi 2**
- Ask the children if they think women have equality today. In what ways can they still see sexism?
- Compare working conditions during the 1960s and 1970s with those of an earlier period. Can the children suggest any reasons for the changes?
   Hi 1/3b, 3c, 4b; Hi 3/3, 4
- Look at the pictures of workers strikes on page 22 in the *Britain Since 1930 Group Discussion Book*.

42/43
Science and invention

Background information

Medicine

Some diseases like smallpox and tuberculosis almost disappeared. Transplants became more common. The first heart transplant was carried out by Dr Christian Barnard in 1967. The period saw increased knowledge about many diseases including cancer and heart diseases, and some preventive medicine. On the negative side it also saw the beginning of Aids.

Farming

To produce more food for an increasing world population, more intensive production methods were introduced like battery farming of hens. New chemicals were introduced to increase the yield of crops.

North Sea oil and gas

New technologies meant that Britain was able to develop oil and gas fields in the North Sea. These proved vital to the economic life of the country. They made Britain less dependent on imports and gave opportunities for export.

Transport and communications

Planes were able to fly more quickly and to carry more people – this made the fares cheaper. The Boeing 747 jumbo jet came into service in the 1970s. It could seat up to 500 people and travel at 1,600 kilometres per hour. Concorde – a joint British/French production – became the world's first supersonic passenger airplane. It first carried passengers in 1976.

In the 1980s Britain became one of the leading nations in the new satellite technologies. Satellite technology meant that television pictures could now be beamed around the world.

As cars and lorries became faster and cheaper so their use increased dramatically. Motorways had to be built. In the 1980s Japanese companies began to build cars in Britain.

Computers and new technology

The early computers could occupy the entire ground floor of an office block. Thanks to the silicon chip, computers have become much smaller and cheaper. Parts of Britain benefited greatly from the manufacture of computers. Computers are now an everyday part of life at home, at school and at work.

Apart from computerisation many other advances have been made. The first pocket calculator was introduced in 1972, and in 1978 Sony introduced their 'Walkman'. In entertainment CD players have been introduced, video players and cameras have become commonplace. Many people have satellite dishes to receive more television channels.

Discussion and activities

- Allow the children to conduct surveys about transport. These might take the form of a traffic count, flow diagrams, surveying types of makes of vehicle, or the number of cars in a family. Following the survey, encourage the children to think about the advances in transport over the last 60 years.   **Ma 5**
- Ask the children to list all the things they use that are computerised. They should include things like shop tills which other people use for them.
- Get the children to think about these questions: If someone who died in the 1930s were to come back to life in the 1990s, what invention might that person think the best or the most surprising? What would they not be surprised to see?   **Hi 1/3a, 4a**
- Get the children to make a frieze of some of the changes in technology from the 1930s to the 1990s.
   Hi 3
- What do the children think would be the most useful invention for the year 2050?
- Look at the photograph of an oil rig on page 21 in the *Britain Since 1930 Group Discussion Book*.
- BLM 18 – Looking at the ways computers have changed the way we live today.

44/45
The environment

Background information

Power pollution

In the 1950s coal was the main form of heating and the main form of power for factories. Chimneys poured smoke into the air. In certain weather conditions this caused terrible smogs. Some London smogs were killers.

The Clean Air Act brought big changes. Many factories switched to electricity. This was generated in coal-generating power stations. The smoke from these was released high into the air. This stopped smog in Britain but the gases helped cause acid rain in Scandinavia. Nuclear power seemed the clean answer. Calder Hill, the world's first nuclear power station, was opened in 1956. Many people are worried about the dangers of nuclear power stations. The Chernobyl disaster of 1986 heightened this awareness.

Water pollution

Thanks to waste products from factories, sludge from sewage and chemical runoffs from agriculture, many rivers were so badly polluted that in many stretches they had no fish. The *Torrey Canyon* oil tanker disaster showed that even the sea and the coastline could become polluted.

Car pollution

With growing numbers of cars, roads became jammed. Gases from cars also caused atmospheric pollution. The lead in petrol was shown to be damaging to children in some city areas.

Healthier living

As people became more aware of health hazards, green politics became more important for all the major political parties. People also made more effort to lead a healthier lifestyle.

Discussion and activities

- Ask the children to debate whether nuclear power is a good or a bad thing. **En 1; Gg 5**
- Make a display of pictures with the children showing pollution problems. Encourage them to choose suitable media – charcoal might be good for depicting smog! **Ar 1**
- The children could make posters that will help draw attention to pollution problems.
- **BLM 19** – Looking at pollutants and how they effect the environment.

Looking back

The key to these pages are the concepts of continuity and change.

Discussion and activities

- Ask the children to put forward their own point of view based on evidence. What do they think has been the most important change over the last 60 years? See if this agrees with the view of an oral history respondent who was alive in 1930.
- Make a 'then and now' display, to illustrate changes which have occurred over the last 60 years.
- **BLM 20** – Finding out about famous people from the period 1930-1990.
- **BLM 21** – Constructing a transport time line.

Key *Britain Since 1930* events

Date	Event
1930-33	The Depression.
1931	The Government introduces the means test.
1936	The Jarrow Crusade. 200 unemployed men march 480km from Jarrow to London.
1939	The Second World War begins.
1940	Winston Churchill becomes Prime Minister.
1940	Rationing begins.
1940	The Battle of Britain (July-September).
1945	The Second World War ends. 8th May 1945 is VE Day. In August the USA drops atomb bombs on Hiroshima and Nagasaki in Japan.
1948	The start of the National Health Service.
1953	Elizabeth II is crowned Queen.
1953	Edmund Hillary and Sherpa Tensing climb Mount Everest.
1954	Rationing ends.
1954	Roger Bannister is the first man to run a mile in under four minutes.
1955	Winston Churchill resigns as Prime Minister.
1956	ITV transmits for the first time.
1962	The *Beatles* have their first hit record – *Love me do*.
1964	Harold Wilson becomes Prime Minister.
1965	Winston Churchill dies.
1966	England wins the World Cup by beating West Germany at Wembley.
1966	The Aberfan disaster. 116 children and 23 adults die when a landslide moves a coal tip onto a school.
1967	The BBC introduces Radio 1 to play non-stop pop music.
1968	The Race Relations Act makes racial discrimination illegal.
1970	The Equal Pay Act.
1973	Britain joins the Common Market.
1975	The Sex Discrimination Act.
1979-1990	Margaret Thatcher is the first woman Prime Minister in Britain.
1984-85	The Miners' Strike.

Further references

Non-fiction

- E. Allen, *Wartime Children 1939-1945*, A&C Black, 1974.
- P. Clark, *Famous Names in Space Exploration*, Wayland, 1978.
- S. Cleeve, *Growing up in the Fifties*, Wayland, 1980.
- L. Coate, *What Was it Like for Children During the Second World War*, Tressell, 1989.
- S. Crawford, *A Family in the Thirties*, Wayland, 1988.
- S. Echlin, *At Home in the 1950s*, Longman, 1983.
- P. Finchan, *The Home Front in the Second World War*, Longman, 1988.
- J. Foster, *A Century of Change: Homes*, Hodder & Stoughton, 1990.
- N. L. Fyson, *Growing up in the Second World War*, Batsford, 1981.
- C. Gilchrist, *People at Work, 1930 to the 1980s*, Batsford, 1983.
- S. Harris, *Life in Britain in the 1950s*, Batsford, 1985.
- C. A. R. Hills, *Growing up in the 1950s*, Batsford, 1983.
- N. Hunter, *Twenty Names in Films*, Wayland, 1989.
- A. Hurst, A *Family in the Fifties*, A&C Black, 1987.
- M. Jones, *Life in Britain in World War II*, Batsford, 1983.
- P. Marshall, *Going Shopping: A history in photographs, 1850s to the present day*, MacDonald, 1984.
- E. Merson, *At Work in the 1930s*, Longman, 1983.
- E. Merson, *Children in the Second World War*, Longman, 1983.
- G. Middleton, *In the Town in the 1930s*, Longman, 1983.
- D. Mondey, *Women of the Air*, Wayland, 1981.
- P. Noble, *A Century of Change: In the street*, Hodder & Stoughton, 1989.
- J. Pascall, *Growing up in the Fifties*, Wayland, 1980.
- J. Pascall, *The Cinema Greats*, Wayland, 1983.
- S. Purkis, *At Home in the 1930s*, Longman, 1983.
- S. Purkis, *At School in the 1930s*, Longman, 1983.
- A. Quinney, *House and Home*, BBC Publications, 1986.
- F. Reynoldson, *War and Home*, Heinemann, 1980.
- F. Reynoldson, *20th Century British History 1919-39*, Heinemann, 1985.
- F. Reynoldson, *20th Century British History 1945 to the 1980s*, Heinemann, 1986.
- N. Richardson, *Life in Britain in the 1960s*, Batsford, 1986.
- S. Robertson, *Famous Names in Films*, Wayland, 1980.
- R. Tames, *Growing up in the 1960s*, Batsford, 1983.
- N. Thompson, *When I was Young: The Sixties*, Franklin Watts, 1990.
- N. Thompson, *When I was Young: The Seventies*, Franklin Watts, 1990.
- N. Thompson, *When I was Young in the Second World War*, Franklin Watts, 1989.
- F. Wilkes, *Growing up Between the Wars*, Batsford, 1979.
- F. Wilkes, *Transport and Travel from 1930 to the 1980s*, Batsford, 1985.

Fiction

The Second World War and 1940s:

- N. Bawden, *Carrie's War*, Gollancz, 1973.
- S. Cooper, *Dawn of Fear*, Chatto and Windus, 1970.
- G. Gifford, *Pete and the Doodlebug and other stories*, Macmillan, 1983.
- M. Magorian, *Goodnight Mister Tom and Back Home*, Puffin 1981.
- J. P. Walsh, *Dolphin Crossing*, Macmillan, 1967.
- J. P. Walsh, *Fireweed*, Macmillan, 1969.

The 1950s:

- L. Berg, *Box for Benny*, Magnet, 1983.
- E. Stucley, *Magnolia Buildings*, Penguin, 1965.

The 1960s onwards:

- M. K. Harris, *Jessica on her own*, Faber and Faber, 1978.
- P. Pearce, *A Dog so Small*, Penguin, 1970.
- K. M. Peyton, *Fly by Night*, Sparrow, 1981.
- J. R. Townsend, *Gumble's Yard*, Viking Kestrel, 1984.

Television

☐ *How We Used to Live 1936-53*, Yorkshire Television.

☐ *How We Used to Live 1954-70*, Yorkshire Television.

Places of interest

There are many interesting visits that can be made when studying the period 'Britain Since 1930'. The following museums have collections relating to the period 1930-90.

☐ Eden Camp, Malton North Yorkshire. A living museum of the Second World War.

☐ Imperial War Museum, London.

☐ Flambards Theme Park, Helston, Cornwall. A re-creation of a street during the Blitz.

☐ National Army Museum, Chelsea, London.

☐ The Design Museum, Butlers Wharf, London.

☐ The Geffrye Museum, London. A museum of English domestic interiors.

☐ Victoria and Albert Museum, London. The dress collection holds a number of fashion items from the 1930 to the 1990s.

☐ Bethnal Green Museum of Childhood, London. This museum holds a wide collection of toys relating to this and earlier periods.

☐ Heritage Motor Museum, Syon Park, Brentford, Middlesex.

☐ Museum of the Moving Image, South Bank, London.

☐ National Railway Museum, Leeman Road, York.

☐ London Transport Museum, Covent Garden, London.

☐ Robert Opie's Packaging Museum, Gloucester. The museum houses a large collection of advertising and packaging, a substantial amount of which relates to the period 1930-1990.

☐ The Cabinet War Rooms, King Charles Street, London.

☐ The Gallery of English Costume, Platt Hall, Rusholme, Manchester.

☐ North West Museum of Science and Industry, Grosvenor Street, Manchester.

☐ National Museum of Wales, Cardiff, South Glamorgan, Wales.

☐ Museum of Transport, Albert Drive, Glasgow, Scotland.

☐ Museum of Childhood, High Street, Edinburgh, Scotland.

☐ The museum of Leathercraft, Northampton. Collections of shoes covering the period, which could prompt a project on fashion.

☐ National Museum of Photography, Film and Television, Prince's View, Bradford, West Yorkshire.

☐ North of England Open Air Museum, Beamish Hall, Stanley, County Durham.

Local history study

The supplementary study unit for local history may be used to study an aspect of the local community during a short period of time, the local community's involvement in a particular event or to illustrate developments taught in other study units. Local history work could therefore be used to complement the work being carried out on the 'Britain since 1930' unit. The obvious links will be through looking at a particular period, such as the war, or through a theme illustrating a development over the period, such as family and domestic life. The National Curriculum non-statutory guidance for history gives a good example of a local history unit concerned with a particular event, the home front in the Second World War, in Section G. The suggested unit in this Resource Book concentrates on family and domestic life over the period by taking views from the 1930s, 1960s and the 1990s.

The range of resources available for a local history study is wide. The local area itself is obviously important and visits can be arranged for the class. Photographs can be taken for comparison with old photographs. Oral history respondents can be contacted through parents and grandparents, through school staff, through local shops and libraries and possibly day centres for the elderly. Other sources will include:

- Maps of your area. The comparison of large-scale maps can reveal a great deal about changing land use. Varying scales can be a problem but careful use of transparencies and an OHP can remedy this.
- Old photographs can be a rich source to investigate change and life since 1930.
- Local newspapers are a rich source of interesting articles and photographs. Ideally you need an approximate date for your enquiry – perhaps gained from an oral history respondent.
- School log books can give an interesting insight into education.
- In some areas writers' co-operatives have encouraged older people to record their memories. These are a very useful source.

Most of these sources are available from the local library or from the local history library or record office. Oral history respondents can be a mine of information and should be encouraged to bring in artefacts that relate to the session they will have with the children. Again parents, grandparents and school staff may have a wide range of sources so it is worth asking!

Example of a local history study

Key issues	Concepts	Content	Sources	Activities	Teaching and learning methods	Assessment questions	Cross-curricular links
• What major changes have occurred in or to the area?	• Continuity and change	• Major changes to land use, development and style of housing	• Maps • Photographs	• Make a time line to show major changes • Make a current land use map	• Teacher presentation • Group work • Field work	• When did it happen? What changes were there? AT 1	Gg
• In what ways have local houses/homes changed?	• Continuity and change • Evidence	• Local housing in the 1930s, 1960s and 1990s	• Photographs • Oral history • Estate agent particulars • Local houses	• List similarities and differences • Explain why changes have occurred • Write estate agent particulars for 1930s, 1960s and 1990s housing	• Group work • Interviewing • Field work	• How are the houses different from each other? • What alterations might have been made since the houses were built? AT 1/3b, 4b • Why were these alterations made?	
• Where and how did the people shop?		• Shopping	• Maps • Pictures/photographs • Oral history	• Conduct a survey of present-day shopping habits. Compare with evidence from the 1930s and 1960s	• Group and individual work • Interviewing	• What changes have there been? AT 1 • How do we know? AT 3	Ma Gg
• How did people transport themselves?	• Communication links	• Transport in 1930s, 1960s and 1990s	• Pictures • Maps • Oral history • Ginn *Pupils' Book*	• Draw forms of transport accompanied by written explanations • Map local transport links	• Group work • Interviewing	• How and why has local transport changed? AT1 • How do we know? AT 3	Gg En Ar

Example of a local history study (continued)

Key issues	Concepts	Content	Sources	Activities	Teaching and learning methods	Assessment questions	Cross-curricular links
• What work did people in the area do? • Did / do men and women do the same work?	• Paid employment • Unpaid employment • Unemployment	• Local occupations	• Oral history • Newspapers	• Make cartoon drawings of people explaining their work	• Group and individual work • Interviewing	• How do we know? AT 3	Ar
• What did people do for leisure?	• Leisure	• Local entertainment	• Oral history • Newspapers • Old films and television programmes • Ginn *Pupils' Book*	• Describe how people used their leisure time	• Group and individual work • Interviewing	• How has leisure time activity changed? AT 1	En
• What did children do? • What was school like?	• Education • Leisure • Toys	• Local schooling, the curriculum, selection, children's games	• Oral history • Old films and television programmes • Log books • Newspapers • Ginn *Pupils' Book*	• Write a diary account of a child's day	• Group and individual work • Interviewing	• How has childhood changed / remained the same? Why? AT 1	En
• What events were celebrated, and how?	• Celebrations	• Coronations, weddings, birthdays, street parties	• Oral history • Newspapers • Photographs • Ginn *Pupils' Book*	• Write an account of a celebration • Make a collage of celebration since 1930	• Group and individual work • Interviewing		En

Blackline Masters

The Blackline Masters extend themes developed in the *Pupils' Book*. They also provide additional forms of evidence to examine. The BLMs therefore encourage children to go back and re-examine the *Pupils' Book*, practise their information book skills, and to read with a purpose.

On each sheet the key skill or concept that the BLM develops is marked at the top. A full explanation of these key skills, and how they can be used as an ideal aid to assessment and record-keeping, can be found in the Key Stage 2 *Teachers' Handbook*.

Symbols are given at the top of some BLMs:

= scissors needed

= glue needed

The table below indicates the following:

- Which Blackline Master relates to each *Britain Since 1930 Pupils' Book* page.
- Which Blackline Master resources different historical perspectives (political/ economic, technological and scientific/ social/ religious/ cultural and aesthetic).
- Which Blackline Master resources aspects of the thematic supplementary study units.

(Valuable time-saving charts showing how *Britain Since 1930* can be linked with the supplementary study units can be found in the Key Stage 2 *Teachers' Handbook*.)

Perspective/theme	2	4	6	8	10	12	14	16	18	20	22	24	26	28	30	32	34	36	38	40	42	44	46
Political				4				9	12							16							
Economic, technical and scientific													13								18	19	
Social																							
Religious																							
Cultural and aesthetic																							
Ships and seafarers																							
Food and farming									10	10													
Houses and places of worship	2																						
Writing and printing																							
Land transport																							21
Domestic life, families and childhood		3		5			7	8	10, 11	10, 11			13	14	15, 17	16	17				18		

Britain since 1930

How do we know what life was like in Britain in the 1930s?

Cut out these pictures and stick them on paper. Write under each picture what the evidence tells us about life in the 1930s.

Draw some more things which help us to find out about the 1930s.

Write an estate agent's description for this 1930s house.
Include details about all the fixtures and fittings.

For Sale

Desirable semi-detached residence

Britain since 1930

Have children's lifestyles changed a lot since the 1930s?
Use the charts to record what you have found out.

favourite toys:_____

_____

comics:_____

_____

leisure activities:_____

_____

school:_____

_____

clothes: _____

_____

other information: _____

_____

1930s children ►

favourite toys:_____

_____

comics:_____

_____

leisure activities:_____

_____

school:_____

_____

clothes:_____

_____

other information:_____

_____

◄ 1990s children

12 Mount Street
Jarrow

1st October 1936

Dear Sir

Your are an unemployed worker in the shipbuilding industry. Write a letter to your local newspaper encouraging other people to join the Jarrow march. Explain why you are going to march and what you hope to achieve.

Britain since 1930

Write a postcard from a 1930s seaside resort describing your holiday.
Include details about your journey, accommodation, and about how
you are spending your time.

During the Second World War people had to carry identity cards.

NUMBER

KBML 297:2

SURNAME *Hagerty*

CHRISTIAN NAMES (first name in full)
Mary

CLASS CODE
A

FULL POSTAL ADDRESS
36 Hillside Road Bradford

HOLDER'S SIGNATURE
Mary Hagerty

CHANGES OF ADDRESS   No entry except by National
Registration Officer, to whom removal must be notified

REMOVED TO (Full Postal Address)
30. Undercliffe Street Bradford

FOR OFFICIAL ENTRY ONLY (apart from Holder's Sig MARKING OR ERASURE IS PUNISHABLE

Design your own identity card for the 1990s.
What information would be important to put on it?

IDENTITY CARD

Britain since 1930

During the war, everyone in Britain was expected to help the war effort.
Describe the following people's work and explain why it was important.

 **Women's Land Army**

_____

_____

_____

 **Coal miner**

_____

_____

_____

 **Air Raid Warden**

_____

_____

_____

 **Home Guard**

_____

_____

_____

 **Fire fighter**

_____

_____

_____

 **Munitions worker**

_____

_____

_____

Which work would you have chosen and why?

_____

_____

_____

List other jobs which you think were important for the war effort.

_____

_____

_____

_____

Britain since 1930

Imagine that you are being evacuated from London during the war. What would you take with you in your suitcase?

Describe your feelings as you went on the platform for the train.

_____

_____

_____

_____

Britain since 1930

Imagine that you are living in London during the Second World War.
Record in your diary what you observed of the German bombing raids.

29th September 1940

The Blitz has continued throughout the winter. What damage have you seen?
How has your way of life been affected?

18th March 1941

Britain since 1930

Cause and effect
Change and continuity
Looking at evidence

Look at this typical week's ration for one person during World War Two.

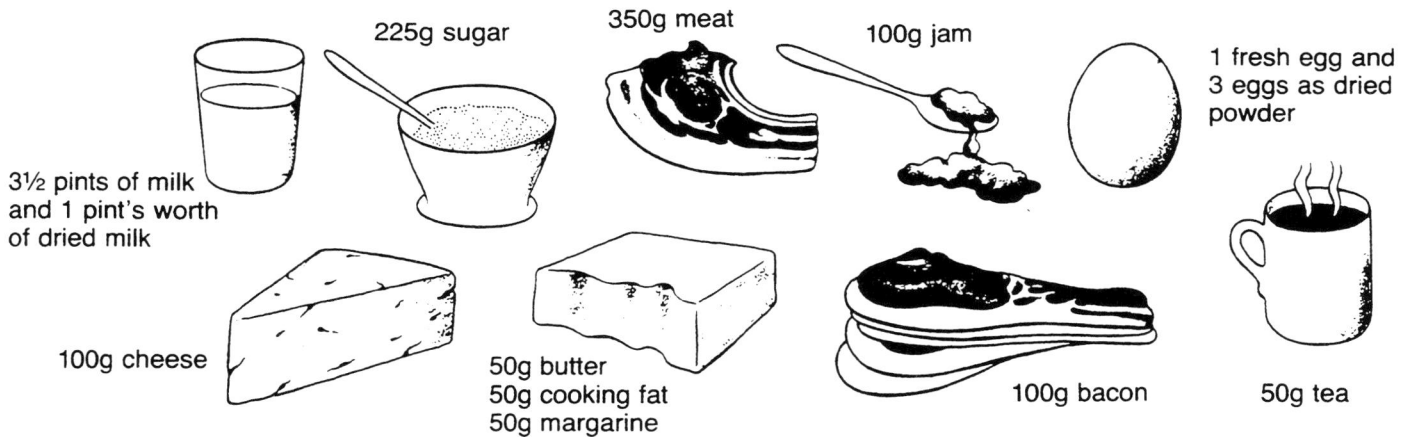

225g sugar
350g meat
100g jam
1 fresh egg and 3 eggs as dried powder

3½ pints of milk and 1 pint's worth of dried milk

100g cheese
50g butter
50g cooking fat
50g margarine
100g bacon
50g tea

Imagine that you are living during World War Two.
There are no frozen foods or convenience foods. You can have as many vegetables as you want. Plan a menu for a week.

	Breakfast	Lunch	Dinner
Monday			
Tuesday			
Wednesday			
Thursday			
Friday			
Saturday			
Sunday			

Work out how much you eat, each week, of the food items below, and compare your quantities with wartime rationing.

	Milk	Eggs	Sugar	Cheese
I eat				
Wartime rationing				

Think about why these foods were rationed.
Make a list of all the reasons you can think of.

Britain since 1930

Clothes were rationed during the Second World War.

shirt
4 coupons

pullover
3 coupons

blazer
8 coupons

handkerchief
½ coupon

scarf
2 coupons

trousers
6 coupons

pair of socks
1 coupon

shoes
3 coupons

blouse
3 coupons

jumper
3 coupons

coat
11 coupons

pair of gloves
2 coupons

skirt
5 coupons

pair of boots
3 coupons

Imagine that you are living during the war. You only have 50 coupons to spend during the year. What clothes would you choose to buy?

Item of clothing	Number of coupons spent	Number of coupons left

How could you increase or vary your existing clothes?

_____

_____

DAILY EXPRESS

No. 14,094   Lighting-up: 9.39 pm to 4.33 am   TUESDAY AUGUST 7 1945   Weather: Cool, showers   One Penny

Smoke hides city 16 hours after greatest secret weapon strikes

THE BOMB THAT HAS CHANGED THE WORLD

Japs told 'Now quit'

THE Allies disclosed last night that they have used against Japan the most fearful device of war yet produced—an atomic bomb.

It was dropped at 20 minutes past midnight, London time, yesterday on the Japanese port and army base of Hiroshima, 190 miles west of Kobe.

The city was blotted out by a cloud of dust and smoke. Sixteen hours later reconnaissance pilots were still waiting for the cloud to lift to let them see what had happened.

The bomb was a last warning. Now leaflets will tell the Japanese what to expect unless their Government surrenders.

So great will be the devastation if they do not surrender that Allied land forces may be able to invade without opposition.

20,000 tons in golf ball

ONE atomic bomb has a destructive force equal to that of 20,000 tons of T.N.T., or five 1,000-plane raids. This terrific power is packed in a space of little more than golf ball size.

Experts estimate that the bomb can destroy anything on the surface in an area of at least two square miles—twice the size of the City of London.

When it was tested after being assembled in a farmhouse in the remote desert of New Mexico, a steel tower used for the experiment vaporised; two men standing nearly six miles away were blown down; blast effect was felt 300 miles away.

And, at Albuquerque, 120 miles away, a blind girl cried "What is that?" when the flash lighted the sky before the explosion could be heard.

Why did the British government support the dropping of the atom bomb on Japan in 1945? Why might some people have objected?
Use the chart to record different points of view.

Points of view	
Supporting the dropping of the atom bomb	Objecting to the dropping of the atom bomb

Britain since 1930

Design an advertisement for a 1950s television set. What points would you include to encourage people to buy?

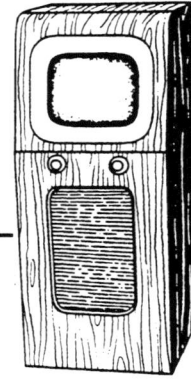

What effects did the increasing popularity of television have on everyday life in the 1950s and 1960s?

_____

_____

_____

Britain since 1930

In 1959 Harold Macmillan said to the British public, "You've never had it so good".
In what ways were the 1950s a more prosperous time for most people?

How do you think these 1950s teenagers might spend their leisure time?

Britain since 1930

The 1960s was a great age for pop music. Teenagers bought many records. Design your own record sleeve for a 1960s pop group.

Britain since 1930

What do you think was the most important reason why the Labour Government supported the introduction of comprehensive schools in the 1960s?
Cut out the boxes and arrange them in order of priority.
Add some of your own reasons in the empty boxes.

The standard of the 11+ exam was not the same in all areas. In some areas it was easier to pass than in others.	Secondary modern schools were not as good as grammar schools.
Children who went to secondary modern schools were less likely to get a good job.	Children should not have to worry about exams when they are only 11.
The 11+ exam mainly tested memory, not intelligence.	All children should have the opportunity of a good education.
Children should be able to go to the same school as their friends.	Children couldn't do interesting work in primary schools, as they had to practise for the 11+ exam.

Compare your arrangement of these boxes with those of your friends.
Are the arrangements all the same?

Britain since 1930

Teenagers developed cults
in the 1950s and 1960s.

Describe what these teenagers
are wearing and how they like
to spend their leisure time.

Rocker

Hippie

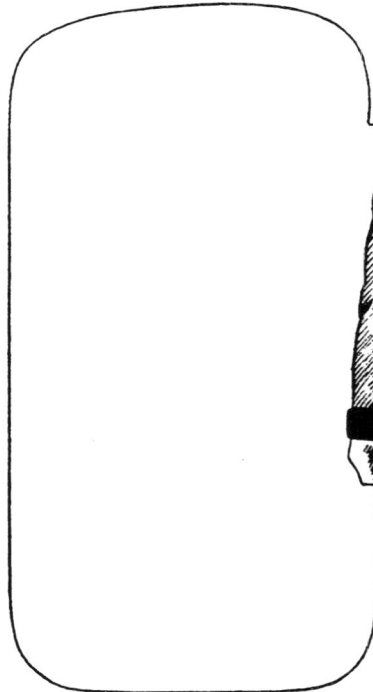

Twiggy

Teddy boy

If you lived in the 1950s or 1960s, who would you choose to be and why?

Britain since 1930

People say that today we live in the 'computer age'. List the areas where computers are used and describe what they have replaced.

Areas where computers are used	What computers have replaced

Do you think that the computer age has improved the quality of everyday life?

_____

_____

_____

Compare your views with those of a friend.

BLM
18

Britain since 1930

Many people are becoming increasingly concerned about the state of the environment and the effects of pollution. Suggest some of the effects which the following might have on the environment.

What measures do you think need to be taken to protect the environment?

Britain since 1930

Why are the following people famous?

Amy Johnson

_____

_____

_____

Elvis Presley

_____

_____

_____

Edmund Hillary

_____

_____

_____

Roger Bannister

_____

_____

_____

William Beveridge

_____

_____

_____

Enid Blyton

_____

_____

_____

Margaret Thatcher

_____

_____

_____

_____

Yuri Gagarin

_____

_____

_____

_____

Place these famous people on a time line. Add other well-known personalities who have lived during the last 60 years to your time line.

BLM
20

Britain since 1930

Cut out the pictures and stick them on a time line, to show how transport has changed over the last 60 years.

Add your own pictures of transport to the time line.

In what ways have people's lives been affected by improved means of transport?